A Secret Room in Fall

Poems by

Maria Terrone

The Ashland Poetry Press
Ashland University
Ashland, Ohio 44805

Acknowledgments are made with gratitude to the editors of the following publications in which these poems first appeared, some published in slightly different versions or with different titles:

Atlanta Review: "Listening to My Husband Describe an 'X-Files' Plot While Driving Past Spring's First Poppies," "A Poet in the Customs House," "Artist 'Anon,'" "The Fruited Plain"
The Comstock Review: "Keep Your Jewelry Safe"
Crab Orchard Review: "My Brother Listens to His Police Scanner," "A Simple Cosmology"
Cream City Review: "The Pedicurists' Club"
Dogwood: "In the Land of Emperors"
Heliotrope: "The Shoot"
The Hudson Review: "The Egyptian Queen Gives Death the Slip," "The Sea Within"
Italian Americana: "The Slain Wife of the Lighthouse Keeper Speaks," "Crisscrossed Shadows"
Notre Dame Review: "The Distance Between Trees," "Rereading the History Book: Centuries XX and XXI," "Guardian Raptors," "Eclipse"
nycBigCityLit.com: "The Load"
Passages North: "Seaside Stonehenge," "Omega Train"
Perihelion: "Allergy Season"
Poet Lore: "Terminal, 1934"
Rattapallax: "A Secret Room in Fall," "The Weather Channel Preacher," "Skin of Mirrors," "The Hunger of the Dead," "O Wanderers"
Rhino: "The Robust Young Man Considers His Burial"
South Dakota Review: "Underground Messengers"
Sou'wester: "Dead Man Riding"
The Spoon River Poetry Review: "Breaking the Code," "How Dolls Are Made"
VIA: "The Glass Factory," "String Theory"
Web del Sol: "Y2K Apocalypse," "The Chairman Speaks Under the Trees"
Willow Review: "For Blanche, Who Named the Colors," "His Cassandra" (2001 Willow Review Award)
Wind: "The Woman Ironing"

"Blood Oranges," "Rosemary," and "White" appear in
*The Milk of Almonds: Italian American Writers on Food and
Culture* (The Feminist Press, 2002; released in paperback, 2003)

"Rapunzel Redux" appears in *The Poets Grimm: 20th Century
Poems from Grimm Fairy Tales* (Story Line Press, 2003)

I am also very grateful to Bibi Wein for her invaluable help in
structuring this collection, and to Martin Mitchell for his support,
generosity, and eagle editorial eye.

Printed in the United States of America

ISBN: 0-912592-60-5

Library of Congress Catalog Card Number: 2006932299

Cover: Georgine Ingber

Photo credit, back cover: Nancy Bareis

For my parents,
Dalio Rotondi (1924–2006)
and Concetta Rotondi

Contents

Four: Urban Messengers

Introduction

Early on in *A Secret Room in Fall*, Maria Terrone says, "So what to make / of these gifts concealed in twisted / tissue? As someone before me has said, / *Beware the fruit of your darkest wishes.*" Poetry, of course, is the gift she gives in this fine second collection, these pages the tissue in which that gift is concealed. All poetry should come with such a warning—we take great risks emotionally, spiritually, culturally, when we write poems and when we read them. They are the fruit, often, of our darkest wishes, but also of our brightest wishes, and their resonance stems from that juxtaposition.

Today, when sincerity and—for lack of a better word—heart seem to be out of vogue in American poetry, a poet such as Maria Terrone seems necessary, timeless. Unlike the current trend of prosaic poetry that uses language like a dull knife, or the glib anecdotal verse that tells a brief story but has no transcendental qualities, or the faux-language poetry that seems to play riddles with the reader, Terrone's finely honed poems are refreshing: accessible but not simple, pleasingly musical, and always satisfying on that visceral level below the surface of the text alone.

For Terrone, poetry itself is *A Secret Room*. Her poems understand the inherent dichotomy of the arts in general, and of poetry in particular: one is alone when one creates it, but one assumes there's an audience. Language implies other, implies communication—and so poetry must become not only a secret room, but has to allow the reader in as well. And then the reader has to be comfortable within. Poems are places of refuge. Of comfort. These poems ask us to come in, to listen, to take a chance reading them. They do not disappoint.

Part of Terrone's ability to please is found in form; fusing traditional forms with free-verse poetics that rely on cadence and rhythm, the poems in *A Secret Room in Fall* feel familiar. They please on the base level of traditions, but their use of such prosody is not heavy-handed in the least; the sonnet that opens the book, "The Egyptian Queen Gives Death the Slip," uses subtle, complex rhymes (my favorite: "stared," "everywhere," "solitaire" and "casket bare"), which exemplify Terrone's linguistic control—her ability to say a lot within the confines of traditional prosody.

"The Egyptian Queen" also exemplifies another aspect of Terrone's work: her choice of subject matter. Terrone moves from persona poems such as this sonnet, to brief narratives looking at others ("The Pedicurists' Club"), to first-person lyrics that capture—the way the best lyrics do—the most resonant moments. But what I particularly like about Terrone's work is how it takes on history and connects the contemporary to the historical but never the esoteric, and connects the lives of others to the life of this speaker and, by association, to the lives of her readers. For instance, in "Glass and Pitcher" she remakes what can be any still life that we'd recognize, and historicizes it:

> Just two objects standing not quite
> side by side in lurid violet—the bruise
> of another morning, the hue of dreams
> that block your air. The table tips
>
> forward, disturbing the planes
> of domestic peace in this still life
> (Paris, '44) where the pitcher salutes
> with its handle, a soldier who's slipped,
>
> unnoticed, into the kitchen. . .

This historical gesture is lovely and risky, and Terrone's eye for specifics makes this a pitcher and glass any of us could have seen.

We see, also, the understatement of Terrone's prosody, the deliberate placement of word beside word, of line break (that second line, "side by side in lurid violet—the bruise," speaks so far beyond the still life, and makes the poem heartbreaking: the two items in the still life empowered suddenly to become two people with the violent "bruise"). Terrone understands the line, and how to create tension within sentences by manipulating her poetic line, while maintaining rhythmic integrity.

Even in her poems that look a little more risky, such as "Rereading the History Book: Centuries XX and XXI," we see Terrone's sense of deliberate lineation and her ability to bring us all in. In this poem, she writes:

> The Dark Ages:
> So many pages of childhood taken up
>   by sleep.
>   Some nights my eyes opened
>   to gray light, a man and woman
>   framed across the alleyway,
> then replaced by a white wall
>   until she returned, or he,
>   to pass through the frame
> alone.

Terrone's lines, although moving across the page à la William Carlos Williams, are deliberate, rhythmically specific, while also enacting the sense of change the poem deals with. And this poem captures that state of pre-adolescence in which the relationships of others—even strangers—beg questions. The "History Book" of the title blurs with the history text of the self—that person who has lived history, and those historical constants that make us all human. She does this without melodramatizing or sentimentalizing. Rather, Terrone wants the image of the poems, the events of the poems, to be the source of dramatic tension, of lyric intensity.

Time and again, Terrone speaks softly, while her poems carry a punch. Undaunted by poetic trends, *A Secret Room in Fall* captures the strength of what a poem can be: accessible but complex, free-ranging but contained, smart without artifice, dramatic without fanfare. The book's final poem, "Underground Messengers," ends in the exotic tempered by the commonplace when she writes: "Those of us who stand / sway to Calypso from the car's far end. / Others nod in sleep, opening messages / washed up on warm, familiar shores." "Calypso" on "familiar shores" says it all. Listen to the kettledrum singing in these pages—those bright sparks of music throughout these poems—and see yourself in a familiar place: this shared space with a shared history. These poems reveal to us why poetry matters as they remind us of our individuality and our shared sense of community.

—GERRY LAFEMINA

One: Distant Signals

The Egyptian Queen Gives Death the Slip

Found: two boxes of wigs in my tomb
and a stash of makeup; considering my rain-
soaked sail to the other side, you assume
a queen needs to freshen up. But no, I changed
looks to slip by unknown in last century's hair style
and dated powder shades like bronze and clay.
You've seen my "death mask" in the museum's Nile
wing by an artist I hired myself. Pray,
do I look dumb or weak? When you stared
into my black-winged eyes, weren't you first to blink?
Taking flight is my talent. Let Death play solitaire,
or else play with *you* his eternal, stinking
game of boredom. That's not for me. I'm everywhere
and nowhere, which is why you found my casket bare.

Forum Romanus

Obelisks, arches, columns, etched
with the names of gods and emperors, lit
like a stage set in the Latin way

to dramatic effect—monuments that anchor me
to this moment while they seem to levitate,
a whole city glowing. Back in the U.S.,

the university's Italian Academy is hosting
a Conference on Randomness. As scholars try
to come to grips with the nature of order

and chance, I stand at this overlook,
in awe that my forebears decided to leave
here, then survived the ocean crossing,

amazed that I survived the flight and can float
on the night with stones and the souls of slaves
who once chiseled, hauled and hefted

each slab onto the next but now roam free
in benign disorder with legions
of wild, unvanquished stars.

The Mad Tea Party

I.

Come, my children!
Such a blue September sky
cannot be ignored.
Let's sip and savor at a table
set outdoors. We'll search
the heavens, our tea leaves,
then pour another cup.
What a glorious day for our party,
what a glorious day
to be alive.

II.

The whistling kettle has turned
to siren.
Who invited these Mad Hatters,
gone completely to pieces,
crashing among us, spewing mayhem?
The morning shatters,
scattering across every ocean.

*After a while the noise
seemed gradually to die away,
till all was dead silence.*

Pulverized concrete furs
our china cups. Nearby, a hand
lies on the sidewalk,
pinky curled.

Someone has murdered time.
Find him, find him!
Off with his head!

Alice, Alice, where are you?

We soon made out we were in a pool
of tears that we had wept.

Alice, where are you?
Fallen down another hole,
but one too deep this time.
We see you smile over and over
from lampposts and stanchions.
Have you seen our girl?
Auburn curls, caterpillar tattoo
on her left shoulder,
butterfly on her right.

We cannot see anything:
even the mirrors have turned their backs,
refusing to let us through. Goodness
gracious, take back this cup,
such ashes, ashes.

How she longed to get out of that dark hall
and wander among those beds of bright flowers
and those cool fountains.

Where are the flowers?
They've fled the garden
and press their petals to cement,
listening for heartbeats.

III.

The invitation drifts on wind,
passes the solemn memos and manifests
that swirl across the roiling river,

and arrives, slightly singed,
in our hands.

The Red Queen requests your company
at a game of croquet.

No, Alice cannot attend.
Please look up her name on your list
and cross it off.

We send our deepest regrets.

Blood Oranges
Provenance: Sicily

Two nails deftly applied to skin expose
an interior life not red—
though that would shock enough—but red
blackened by the color of blood spilled
and dried in history's shadow.

You would expect a thousand years
of conquest to produce a bitter
taste. Then how can this sweetness
be? *Beware of strangers,*
my mother warned, joined

by her parents' blood to a sun-blinded isle
of secrets. *Never trust appearances.*
The Sirens were enchanting,
bird legs and claws hidden
behind long hair that blew glorious

as their song over the Straits of Messina.
Sometimes, when fierce currents
force up the deepest dwellers,
their phosphorescence makes the sea
a silver lure to ensnare unwary

travelers—one more *Fata Morgana*
in a place that loves mirage. So what to make
of these gifts concealed in twisted
tissue? As someone before me has said,
Beware the fruit of your darkest wishes.

Listening to My Husband Describe an "X-Files" Plot While Driving Past Spring's First Poppies

It is all a conspiracy.

See how their heads bend
at the same angle, picking up my thoughts
as they escape this metal cage into the wind.

What you mistake for stamens are antennas
tuned to frequencies beyond our understanding. Why
do they sprinkle the tender earth
      like droplets of blood?
And where do they come from?
      Underground.

They plotted the past year in cells
no light could penetrate, and now
they've arrived, spreading over our land

with a shocking beauty that will seduce,
then hypnotize. They got Dorothy from Kansas—
I read the file. The story we know
was a sham; that sweet kid was haunted
for life. They'll get us, too,
following orders from the mole who sent them—
the hunched one in the overcoat, smoking,
without a face.

My Brother Listens to His Police Scanner

Trapped voices escape from Bob's earphones.
Just down from Vermont, he rests
on the guestroom sofa, plugged into
heart attacks and drug busts,
drunk drivers, domestic brawls, an unbalanced
man on the ledge of the Triboro Bridge.
For hours, he eavesdrops on the city
then calls, *There's a hold-up*
in progress almost next door, yanking
out the jack so that I too can be tuned
to the local frequency, get to know my neighbors.
The dispatcher's call for back-up crackles
in our room like fire drawing near.
But when I glance at the garden below,
the trees of late summer seem fearless,
their deep, even breath like the speech
of yogic masters. In the north country,
leaves like spent tongues
have already begun to fall, whole forests
practicing for their long silence.

The Glass Factory

Morals in the glass factories are proverbially bad.
—an inspector's comment, caption to a 1908 Lewis Hines photo

Even a decent girl can hide nothing here.
I see the boys and even the old ones
stare at my smock, then my eyes, as if they can see ·
clean through. It's mighty dangerous, too.

If a body's not careful, you can get scraped
by sand, burned, or cut real bad.
Between the boys and the heat
and the broken glass, I tried to carry myself

as if I was a babe wrapped tight
in one of the thick quilts ma makes.
They still stared—maybe even more—
and I got tired trying to hold back.

The words they say to me! Even with the furnace
roaring, they whisper against my ear till
I feel something taking shape inside me,
first soft as taffy, then sparkling like the glass beast

I saw a man make once, blowing through his lips.
I want to keep their words like the preserves
that will fill these jars so I can take them out
next year when I turn 14, and I'm feeling old.

The Slain Wife of the Lighthouse Keeper Speaks

He wearied of my piano playing—
I so loved that sonata!—
the way it echoed against the stone stairs
and spiraled out the eye of our house
like another kind of light.
I played often and loud till my groom
took an axe to the keys,
then me. Others called him Monster
and made him pay, but I don't mind:
this 20-year-old will not know gray
or black and blue. And yet. . . you stare
at my hair, red forever undone in the moment
of wildest music and surprise;
pity me my stained shirtwaist, a century old
this day. In truth, I envy you:
your fickle heart that hums so many tunes,
even your bruises, alive in their changing hues.

Before the Storm

The wind hisses then shrieks
missing the missing,
the names on walls the names
about to be inscribed   forever
the unknowable
nameless

It keens to a dry-eyed sky
sweeps asphalt court running track
lovers' path   Calm now
it whispers to the field
where students in sweats
and baseball caps strolled
tenderly strokes their afterimage,
their wake of displaced air   lingering
tang of musk and citrus

          Now the siren wind:
another fire erupts
in another precinct of the heart
a crime has been committed
in the name of love   an iron gate
bangs shut and someone's heart
hugs the bars of solitary
confinement   Violence
has been done quick call 911
the heart of that heart
is missing.

A Secret Room in Fall

From a chair beneath the oak tree,
you see minarets
in the leaves' shadows,
acorns like onion domes, a few drops
of gold light splashing through

like a revelation:
summer is over. Farewell
to motives transparent
as glass and the blankness of mind
you mistook for enlightenment.

Cardinals and blue jays at your feet
are weaving a pattern fluid
as a Persian carpet that you must ride
deep into the maze named Fall.
Behind unmarked doors

expatriates from summer who fled
years ago are propped against pillows
in the permanent amber haze
of back rooms. They'll serve
mint tea steeped black, whispering

that you, too, can make a home
in this once dazzling quarter
always on the verge
of corruption. There are worse places
to live with your secrets.

So take the tea, their tips, the keys
to your own concealment.
Even now, plots have been hatched
and scouts fan out
from the winter palace.

Breaking the Code

White rain drips in dots and dashes;
falls from the eaves like a shower curtain
you can see through, barely, and beyond,
green arms raised in warning or welcome—
you don't know which, you
in that white wicker chair (rented cottage, holes

of knotty pine), watching chipmunks vanish
between rocks. Birds, laughing, know something
you don't, and there's a whistling far off,
a signal you may be missing—you can't know
sitting there, facing the rain and a thousand poems
you haven't read—you, there! with that razor blade

in one hand raised above your magazines,
trying to decipher what lies beyond
the words, within each sound,
which messengers arrived too late
or were never meant for you, which ones
must be pulled from the heap, still breathing.

Two: Freeze Frames

A Poet in the Customs House

Pleased by my jottings, the President
found me employment. Now
I work in a civic temple on a tongue
of land that speaks the Babel
of ivory tusks, bolts of silk, cinnamon
and jasmine tea, each item to be weighed,
counted, and assessed in the definitive language
of ledgers, my eye trained to detect,
then reject, what's tainted,
too dangerous to wave through.
While merchants line up to pay,
my mind wanders across its Bosporus
of time. Today, a lamb's wool shawl
trussed me in childhood till the sweat
began to pour; yesterday, a crystal vial released
a musky night I thought I'd stoppered.
On breaks, I need to gaze on the black,
opaque sea, breathing deeply.
But then another ship appears,
bearing poems I can't appraise
among its dense, resplendent cargo.

Artist "Anon"

1. Embroiderer of the Emperor's Robes

Summoned as a boy, he stays alive
in the Forbidden City by weaving
memories with the silk of his mother's hair,
green thread of mountain mornings.
I squint before its dazzle,
searching for the old, conscripted tailor.
He hides, a bent shadow
on the retinue's fringe, spent eyes
narrowing to the eye of his needle.

2. Etcher of Scrimshaw

Exiled sailor,
a fallen-down drunk lassoed
by deck rope, tossed by anger's maelstrom.
But when sunk in loneliness,
he conjures wife and son
on bone: amazing,
how the homesick heart
can guide the improbable hand
to this precise and spidery black art.

3. Itinerant Painter

He travels the Roman Empire by cart
and foot, grinding purple seashells,
gathering soil, soot, and chalk, crushing
colored stones. The names of senators,
centurions and prosperous olive merchants
are lost in time. Yet century after century
his subjects gaze with all-knowing eyes,
familiar to each generation. The faceless

painter? Returned to his element,
he can be found everywhere:
in shell, soil, soot, chalk, stone.

4. Immigrant Seamstress

And what of the girl whom steerage
nearly tore to tatters?
All the doors are locked and exits blocked
in her new country of sorrow.
Even in waning light, she bends
to stitch ten thousand jet beads
onto this black opera cloak
for a patron of the arts
whose name we still revere.
Unfurled on the scarred workbench,
it reminds her of the starlings—
the way hundreds, flashing iridescence,
would swoop down, then settle,
on the rocky fields back home.

The Weather Channel Preacher

A man struck by lightning
    survives,
tells of awakening,
    thirty feet from where
he stood, fishing,
    to a hole in his shirt,
singed skin just above
    the heart.
Dumb-struck, awe-struck,
    knocked-off-your-horse struck,
he preaches now about this
    Higher Power,
tries to save others.
    He's a large man
with hair curly as a lamb's,
    and black eyes
fixed in the fathomless
    moment after his burning.

Y2K Apocalypse
—a 1999 New Year's Day musing

The speckled blue cave of the self-
cleaning oven crackles
like a robin's egg breaking open.
On this day of fresh starts,
I want to believe in our dominion
over animate and inanimate worlds,
that by simple commands, we can erase
the mess we've made.

Last night Raffaello painted a Doomsday scene—
plane crashes, penury and darkness—
as our electronic guardians fail us, crashing
one by one like proud angels,
damned. Sipping champagne, I struggled
to imagine this day next year,
warming hoarded cans of soup
over a log fire.

Now, deep within our apartment,
you're tapping on computer keys.
From time to time, a single drumbeat
signals mistakes, each aborted
attempt to defy the program.
A smoke detector begins to bleat,
then shriek like a fatted calf remembering
its own death, this blast of heat,

the final rendering to charred remains.
All is preordained: after three hours
our kitchen crucible shines
like an enamel icon,
its luminous face
counting down.

Terminal, 1934

Standing motionless as chess pieces
in huge granite squares—
    4:20 by the clock atop the ticket booth—
the travelers crane their necks,

    watching for a sign. A thin man
hugs a twine-cinched box to his chest.
    Couples in the photo clutch hands,
necks straining at the same angle.

    In hats and worn topcoats,
buffed shoes and hand-me-down suits,
    the adults stare high above, as if
there were no ceiling, only sky, no coming

    or going, just this cold cathedral vigil.
The boys and girls look elsewhere.
    Stopped in the middle of childhood,
contracted by the weight of others' longing,

    they search their parents' faces.
It is getting late; gaunt shadows
    stretch across the floor. Massed
in a gray clot at the bottom

    of a grand staircase or spaced evenly
against limestone walls,
    the people keep their eyes raised,
waiting for word of their release.

The Shoot

Grackles swoop down, then spread
like a black cape around my brother's house.
My brother is kind to animals,
shoots at nothing but one man—
a perp line-drawn on paper, plucked
from his basement arsenal. I see that face
in fields of feverfew, pock-marked
by bullet holes.

When we meet, we never flout the rules,
avoid politics, the N.R.A., or why
a teacher would become a cop
in middle age. Instead, we hike his woods,
past ancient cars pushed down a ravine
by agents unknown. Their shapes shift
and sink, a growing mystery
in the forest bed. As we stroll the abandoned
road, I'll note its widening rift,

the new guns. *This one's a 22*,
my brother says and cocks his head,
making room for mine.
The scope snags a woodchuck
and bees that cling to raspberry fuzz.
One by one, the residents of his kingdom
pass through the cross hairs unharmed,
and yet I recoil when Bob takes aim.

He squeezes the trigger:
The cape explodes into shadow
that covers us both, then shreds to tatters
headed for my heart's chamber.

The Pedicurists' Club

When the pedicurists meet, it's always
someplace off the beaten track, with a private
room in back where shoes can be shed
among friends. They talk shop: the price
of cotton wads, a new exercise to steady the hand.
But mostly the pedicurists delight in one another.
They handle the cutlery like surgeons' tools,
inspect for rough edges, buff with their napkins
before picking at a meal of legless chicken.
Afterward, they take turns shaping and polishing
words to best describe their feelings.
"Our comedown," Darlene once said to nods
around the table, for all knew the pain
of painting ten brilliant miniatures at a clip
that are shoved into the dank, then chipped
into oblivion. Like confessors, the pedicurists
are exposed to daily poisons, secret
festering gnarls, but remain immune, devout
believers in self-improvement. In truth,
they're romantics who perceive the shining
potential of dull surfaces, ordinary
things. At night, when their meetings
end, the pedicurists always exclaim
over the Passion Pink sky, its clusters
of ten crescent moons "like commas,"
Darlene declared. And recalling grammar
taught long ago, they pause
and pause again, tingling before such perfection.

The Distance Between Trees
—at the Edward Steichen photo exhibit, Whitney Museum, New York City

A modern man, he allowed himself
one small, chemical intrusion and fixed
a bar of light above groves somber as the century
just passed. The trees he let be, huddled in a blur
of sleep and tangled limbs, the brooding, charcoal
air. I'd like to leave him there, conjuring dawn
in his lab, before he learned how to arrange
shadow so artfully, to buff the whites of starlets' eyes
till they gleamed, dangerous as pearls that lure
divers to depths of the South Seas. Before
he shot ads for face soap called "filtered sunshine"
and posed Paris models inside mirrored triptychs.

At the end, turning to a single shad-blow tree
beyond his window, he gives us a tired ghost
bleached to abstraction, branches scratching out
their unsteady calligraphy. In other photos,
he's heightened the leaves' color, and they seem
to hover like stoplights above blacktop, the deep
foreground of his driveway. It's the mid-sixties,
suburban Connecticut, and it's raining.

For Blanche, Who Named the Colors

Praise Blanche, who lived alone
in a ground-floor flat
but dwelled in kingdoms

of Venetian Marble and Antique Pearl.
Pondering colors
for the paint company,
she discovered each one's soul

and gave them their names
when we might say
Rose is just rose or
These shades are all the same.

Praise Blanche, who retreated
behind Cubicle Gray for days
to meditate on lilac till we feared
a plunge into monochrome.

When she emerged,
face flushed, her voice was a bell
extolling *Silver Chalice!*
First Light! Ice Ballet!

each shade a stand
against sorrow and pain,
the void of no-names,
even when the tongue quavered

and came to rest, remembering
someone in palest Lauren's Lace.

White

After dinner, my cousin Ron offers
white peaches and white cherries, the sweetest,
most costly kind. The sun is dropping
like a fat yolk into the bowl
of woods that surround his new house
while we plan the summer days ahead,
pressing our luck as we might test
a fruit's ripeness, hoping we'll taste
perfection.

So hard to believe he'll soon turn sixty.
Twenty-five years ago, seeking
Maine's simple life, he came to hate
that state where nothing grows
for long. Even berries were puny,
he said, covering the land like buckshot,
staining skin with the devil's blue ink.
But mostly he came to hate the gluttony
of white that long, jobless winter—how
it gulped at windows but wanted more
than glass, devouring space, time, his faith
in his own senses; white that billowed
like priests' robes, then felled trees,
killing power and a man at his stove
who wasn't found for a week.

The room darkens.
In two years, I retire, Ron says,
lots of time to catch a record-breaking striper,
to cook more meals like this one.
He'll put behind the years of teaching,
the restaurant that almost ate him alive,
the Christmas Eve spent selling trees
in a frozen city lot. I watch
the pits accumulate on his plate,

only the barest shreds still clinging
to the spots he could not
scrape clean.

Rosemary

Grow it for two ends, it matters not at all
Be if for my bridall, or my burial.
— Robert Herrick

Wreathed in the herb's scent of sea and pine,
my two aunts leaned over the uncooked lamb,
dabbing blood from the stainless pan
gently, as if to nurse a wound. Words twined,
sometimes tangled across the tabletop like vines
in Italian hills where they played, girls not yet stunned
by the climb into new lives. They were orphans
disguised as grown women, tending the shrine
of the past until their memories became my own
Paradise Lost (and Gained, to know that once, in spring,
sky inclined to earth as rosemary's blue flowers).
Aunts Sarah and Anna signed *X* over and over
the lamb's flesh: I see a flash of knives and wedding rings,
nettles pressed deep, to keep the taste of those hours.

The Woman Ironing

Fourteenth summer in Nancy's backyard
on her creaky glider under the ginkgo tree,
the muggy night pressing down
like a strict parent, but we're easing
back and forth over the books,
the boys, the longing, the restless
leaves stirring and sighing,
their pleated fans rustling applause
to "Eleanor Rigby" in two-part harmony
sung over spurts of baseball static
from a halting kitchen radio,
the driveway behind our tidy little
houses a long stretch of tar still
sticky even in the dark on this square block
where a person may live
for years and one day come upon
herself as if awakening at a mirror,
like the woman we saw ironing all summer
at her apartment window who faced out
but never looked up, the weary
woman who stood, still ironing at dawn
when we glanced her way after a night spent
watching old movies and imagining
our future.

Flood Lines

Rain, five days straight:
   we scurry into candle shops
      where wind chimes go mad,

clanging a New Age of Water.
   The gray Vermont inn turns sinister,
      a pewter tankard leeching

poison into pilgrims' veins.
   In the growing must of our room,
      we trace whirlpools

in a bureau's oak grain, study
   the claw-foot tub's rusty excretions,
      beetle-typeface of grotesquely

swollen books, until black runes
   crawl out to float, belly-up, in our faces.
      Such rot in the air! Such dead weight,

when every word we exchange
   is examined like a statue
      hauled up from the deep in chains.

Even now when the sun
   sprinkles droplets of light
      through the inn's lace curtain

and across this page, these words,
   like moving floodlines, record
      one summer's rising peril.

Three: Eyes Sealed Open

String Theory

The world's not constructed of particles but tiny loops, say the String Theorists.
This is their Holy Grail, the big idea unifying all natural forces. They worked
at warp speed, but the loose ends weren't tied in time for the new
millennium. My theory: the world's a giant spool of string
unraveling since Day One. When we're tangled
by problems, stomachs in knots, the string
has caught on cosmic debris. Turning
within, medievalists found meaning
in phlegm, blood, bile; but now,
sensing that we merely reflect
what's outside, we say we're
strung out. In the riotous '60s,
as the string snagged again & again,
nervous hands tied macrame that almost
strangled the world. Sometimes, our days roll
out smoothly. The earth's spin pulls us from our beds,
snipping the threads of dreams. We scatter to work, laugh;
kick off our shoes at the end of each day. The world unwinds too,
and together we inch towards the untethered space beyond our last turn.

Skin of Mirrors

Driving to the bay,
we pass corporate parks,
high rises curved like the bows
of cruise ships anchored
in a concrete sea.
Potatoes once grew there,
roots tangled like ropes
of seaweed, black eyes
facing down: deeper, an Indian
burial ground. The buildings
       in their skin

of aqua-tinted mirrors
exchange glares,
self-reflections of the mighty
who need not
say more. Talk to me.
Sometimes I feel I'm a skater
skimming the frozen surface
of my own life, each mark I make
vanishing behind me.
       Your hand

steers us over waves
of highway. Sensing my gaze,
you turn, dark lenses sending my face
back to me like a shrunken
sister-creature met
inside sleep's cave.
Later, gulls line the shore's edge,
staring into the glassy water,
bewitched princes
hungry to return
       to themselves.

His Cassandra

Pilate's wife sent a message:
Do not interfere in the case of that holy man.
I had a dream about him today which has greatly upset me.
    —The Gospel of St. Matthew

He ruled, but I had his ear—
mine attuned to stirrings and murmur,
betrayal that could rise like a swarm of wasps.
And my eyes saw what his could not.
He called me his Cassandra and half-believed.
Each morning as he left, he smiled and kissed
my brow still beating
from visions that shook me
sole to skull:
sun plunging through sky, water climbing
up our doorway, a legion of horses rearing.

I did not ask to awaken that day to howling,
to see that strange one stand
before my husband, who washed
his own hands in a blood-steeped bowl.

That vision never left me.
Soon after, Pilate did—
said he needed a woman
who had no dreams.

The Tour Guide of Pompeii

reaches down,
scoops the ground,
hands a craggy white nugget
to each woman in the group.

This is what buried the city, he says.
Not lava, but pumice,
and of course, poisonous gas.

Moments before, he'd led us
through the heat and dust to view
a glass-encased body,
contorted hands raised
to what had been a face.

The rock feels lighter than air.
Some of us weigh it in our palms,
peer closely, then let it drop.
Others cover the means of destruction
with handkerchiefs to be unwrapped,
carefully, at home.

The Sea Within

Rain, sleet, snow and back this Christmas day.
Then there is the matter of dissolution,
ice blowing at right angles and I'm waiting
at the window for a close-up look,
but rain smears the pane, there's a ghost
of a sparkle at the watery edge, then that too is gone.
Snow Queen's nervous breakdown, a crying jag.

Dad doesn't know where he is.
Mother is trying to show him how
to sit down on the chair. I set the table with white
heirloom linen, tatting like snow crystals, silver
spoons that cup our startled faces.
I remember my father feeding me
as he read a fairy tale, the miracle of the princess
who wakes from a deep sleep
when they'd given her up for dead. You think
the body is immutable, the mind will always spin,
a brilliant kaleidoscope, the sea we hold within
will allow us to sail through our own lives,
unharmed.

Look out: pummeling of ice now,
mounds big enough to sink every fabled ship.
Ice everywhere: even the smallest bushes
have turned to spears. Mother picks up a knife
to cut his food. The spears in the garden soften,
then weep, bandaged, within minutes,
by snow that rises in a sudden updraft
like flung confetti in the instant before it falls.

A Simple Cosmology

I. August 21, 2001

A week after the silent attack
beneath the maple tree, the sidewalk stain
has faded from our super's bleach,
brush, and rain.

Someone carried off
the photo and vigil candles,
leaving wax to seal the ground
like a letter his friends don't need to open now,
knowing the last lines.

I've watched shopping carts and roller blades cross
that concrete slab.
A child pulling a toy wagon.
Chinese restaurant workers pedaling
to the next delivery, uniforms white
as priests' robes.
And New York detectives in pairs,
avuncular, who paced the spot, pressing cards
into my hand, urging me to stay in touch:
all the wheels turning.

II. Early December

The last constellation of leaves
lies like jagged stars.
What did I expect this season of grief
but the usual turning?

One person here never made it home;
then across the river, thousands.
Thousands of candle flames shook

at the sky, demanding to know where
they'd vanished.

Voids may hold life inside the rubble,
experts said, trying to conjure hope
from nothing.
So they dug and confirmed our fears:
nothing still equals nothing.

If I lived in another time,
I'd find divine design in every death
by plague or arrow,
I'd draw lines through the teeming sky
to summon centaur and archer,
all the gods would point the way.

My cosmology is simple: at the center
of the universe are these tangled boughs,
a cat's cradle rocking against a cold
alabaster sky; at the end of one branch,
this spare scattering of gold.

I want to name the shape of what remains
"Cup of Mercy Major"
and use its light to trace
every son and daughter lost
in the tumult, to call forth eyes, ears, lips,
every shining face.

How Dolls Are Made

At 18, partly formed, confident
in the possibility of my own perfection,
I was drawn by a machine hum
down a narrow street to that doorway:
boxes of heads, bins of torsos,
and the night shift factory workers,
all men, silent, who sliced away
the excess plastic from the bodies
like bargain-basement doctors busy at
liposuction. I watch the tiny figure
of myself watch, in fascination, men
who didn't know they spoke to me,
carving arms still warm from molds
with stubby knives, flinging heads streaming
Rapunzel-like hair into cardboard turrets.
I see my glassy eyes open and close,
then blink back real tears.
I see myself shrink back, and back
to my first doll, a hug of rubber
consolation against some childhood sorrow,
recalling at that threshold
the first sense of self in pieces,
a girl-child to be assembled
and shaped by many hands.

Rereading the History Book:
Centuries XX and XXI

The Dark Ages:
So many pages of childhood taken up
        by sleep.
    Some nights my eyes opened
        to gray light, a man and woman
                framed across the alleyway,
then replaced by a white wall
        until she returned, or he,
        to pass through the frame
alone. The satin slip she wore
        crisscrossing
    their room left an afterglow,
            a white X
stamped behind my eyes: do not
        read this text.

                Skip to

The Nuclear Age.
Page after page of warnings:
        Beware of chromosome X,
            aberrant.
Double X makes female,
                double-crossing Eve.
    A blue X marks the spot
where they blast your breast
                with that invisible
        skull and crossbones.
        You're sick,
so these rays may cure you;
        If x, then y:
    fossilized logic unearthed
from the Age of Reason.

The Room Between Light and Sleep

From our bed, I hear the clicks
you make in the living room
as you twist the lamps' plastic tongues
to silence their blaring light.

My uncle didn't know I stood
just outside his hospital room,
moving my right foot into the glare,
then back, his throat clicking like tracks
before a train thunders through.

Other nights, it's I who stands alone
in the black lake of our living
room, amazed to be alive
and walking on the stilled waves
of a wood-grained floor.

Even from the door I could see
the crystal spheres that dripped
one by one into his veins,
their seductive beauty.

Sometimes I dip my head
to the narcotic potpourri of lilac leaves,
sip from the pearl cup
we bought on some trip to paradise,
before feeling my way back to you.

I never entered his room.
In gowns of blinding white,
nurses had encircled him,
and I thought he was asleep.

Sky Full of Hands

What to make of the open, hopeful palms
of leaves in their descent,

some touching midair, or rushing together
on the ground in a blast of wind,

a massive rally of congregants
trying to raise themselves from the dead,

but here and there, a single survivor,
a brilliant leaf still clinging to the tree

like a red flag high above small, curled fingers,
and what to make of their loud sighs

this windy night, the nervous breathing out,
not in? Yesterday came news of a tsunami:

for miles, nothing but an ocean wall
and a sky full of hands.

Resurrection in an Initial "R"

*Title of an illuminated manuscript page from the Choir Books of the
Church of San Georgio Maggiore, Venice, 1467–70*

I rise daily, a miracle.

They say you cannot dream
   you die
but I've come close
  in my Lazarus cave
called sleep.

Still I unwind myself
  from a tourniquet of sheets,
push back the stone,
 fly up to the light
and a choir of robins—

they've got that
   Alive and Sing
routine down pat,
   that tremolo of throat,
wing-beat-back-the-night,

 that bloody resurrection.

California

I. Flight

This is what it feels like to be a god:
to hover fearless at the edge of space,
far from tangled roots,
the downward pull of No.
Before you lies creation:
clay tiles the color of burnt sienna
reach to the vanishing point,
sun glazed—
the earth's roof of fire.

II. Gerstle Cove

A black swan
  dips its head, a tree trunk bent
    to water; seals wobble offshore

like spilled mercury. If
  I think your eyes
    are stone markers,

the fog that blurs all borders
  rebuts. *You've been erased.*
    There is nothing here to mark.

There is no speech.
  Only surf and wind
    carving messages into cliffs

and the plea of my outstretched
  hand trying to grasp yours,
    trying to grasp the why and where

of what slips away. Years later,
    we'll search for their coordinates
        on the map of memory.

III. Fort Ross, a Russian outpost on the Northern coast, 1837

On clear days, Elena can't think.
But when Pacific fog, dark and salty,
breaches the fort's walls,
her head clears as it used to
after a nip of caviar, sip of icy vodka.
She's back in her carriage,
Moscow streets rolling past.

She sees each door and dome,
park and parapet glint like crystal,
the glowing faces of Vladimir and Anna,
even the strangers on shore
who waved rags as the ship moaned
and she squeezed the hands
of her children so hard,
they screamed.

A bird thumps the pane.
Elena opens her eyes,
notices every window is a door
painted gray. She rushes out
to her summer garden, snowblind,
and wonders if she's alive.

IV. Fern Canyon

On this day of sun and cloud,

    a thousand shades of green

make a thousand shades of light

that tint my skin,

imprint my body

　with leaves and ferns

until I am a living paradox—

　a fossil that keeps changing

as I shift within

　the green embrace

of two rippling walls.

V. San Francisco

City of uncertainty, of why, what if,
where the fissure in my heart grows.

Walking the unfamiliar streets,
I come upon a glassed-in carousel:
fierce horses bob up and down, riderless,
their manes windblown, propelled
by an unseen force. Teeth bared, they ride
the gyre, the terrifying silence.

The aquarium's flickering blue light lulls
like a late night t.v. screen
pulling you into a dream.
Angelfish glide by,
the inky letters of an ancient language
moving across a page
in curlicued dance, drawing me deep
inside their radiance.
A tank encircles the Great Hall.
I stand in the center, mesmerized

by hundreds of silver fish swimming 'round
in slow motion, a few darting out
like sparks from a single giant wheel.

After the last guard shuts
the last light and the visitors
have gone home to feed, I think
of that silver wheel turning, long after
we've left for another coast, caught
once more in the reefs
of our discontent, I think of that wheel
revolving unseen, in the black hum.

The Chairman Speaks Under the Trees

Was it his breath
that made the leaves shift?
I could see them twist,
little hearts of polished green
forced to reveal
a gray underside. Their shadows
muddied the Chairman's face
and he narrowed his eyes, struggling
to see from ours.

Blotches spread across his fine suit:
He seemed to have tumbled down
a dried-up well,
his brow lined with remains
of rotting twigs.
But his diamond ring bore
a hole through the shadow,
reminding us he'd gathered our hopeful
pennies before he inched back up.

Glass and Pitcher

As master of the veiled reference, Picasso said, "Even casseroles can scream."
—Curator's comment, Fogg Museum, Boston

Just two objects standing not quite
side by side in lurid violet—the bruise
of another morning, the hue of dreams
that block your air. The table tips

forward, disturbing the planes
of domestic peace in this still life
(Paris, '44) where the pitcher salutes
with its handle, a soldier who's slipped,

unnoticed, into the kitchen. An empty
water glass seems to waver, unable
to hide itself or harbor secrets—
a vessel waiting to be gripped, used,

smashed. Outside the unseen door,
commandants of the Third Reich
snap to life in cafés,
demanding their bread and knives.

Seaside Stonehenge

You saw them in a news photo
with a clever headline—
t.v. sets that washed ashore—
but you feel compelled
to take them seriously; in fact,
you see yourself alone at dusk
walking through this Stonehenge
encircled by pebbles, charred wood chips
scraping your bare feet,
the air filled with static
from the sound of foam that breaks
on seaweed, then recedes.

The screens face one another
or stare east across the ocean
from where they came,
antenna folded—as if betrayed
by evolution, encased
in a plastic carapace
like bugs too big to crawl away
that once held the world
in a single glassy eye.

Allergy Season

This is the season of tears
     that appear without sorrow.
First they curve April's green spikes,

then you see as after a rain,
     a painful glistening, silver coins
flung at a beggar's face.

And that itch you cannot reach:
     Why should it be otherwise
when everything you see

is unattainable:
     treetops, sky, your own longings
buried in their seed.

Crisscrossed Shadows

Love, let's learn to temper
this craving for symmetry, resist
the force that propels us from room to room,
squaring pillows, aligning window shades,
and prizing, above all,
the balanced exchange.

I ask one more thing: please
don't try to straighten

what's askew

in me—the occasional slump or down-turned

mouth and what might seem my oblique
rendering of nightly dreams
from *The Cabinet of Dr. Caligari.*

Let's celebrate the state
where even the most upright lean
like drunks, and bodies

      make crisscrossed
shadows that serrate
      the flat, complacent night.

The Hunger of the Dead

When I feel the ice
of their lifeless eyes piercing
the sky's black drape,

I pity the dead. I pity
their eternal hunger
for all that's left behind,

how every night they gnaw
the darkness
trying to find a way back.

I pity their boredom
in light everlasting, the dazzle
that blinds, then seals

their eyes open.
If only we could see
how futile it is to thumb closed

the lids of the newly dead,
to draw a white curtain
around them.

Four: Urban Messengers

In the Land of Emperors

He's alive, but halved, on a plank—
head, torso and muscled arms
wheeling down the train platform
to the top of the stairs,
and I stop in my tracks
midway through some rumination
that's instantly replaced by one
about humans made in God's own image.
I imagine the workbench abandoned
in the middle of the job,
some more cursed than others,
forced to eat dust,
denied the chance to run.
I reverse my steps,
read a billboard, wait till it's safe: he's gone.
Still, my legs quiver
on the same steep flight of steel steps
he bumped or slid or rode down
a moment ago, transporting himself
to the next plane, the broken world.
In marble halls, I've admired
the busts of emperors, larger than life
with their smashed noses and missing limbs.
I know a black king
glides by now on ball bearings,
past sidewalk crowds that part in two.

Guardian Raptors

More than three million migratory birds. . . bald eagles and raptors. . .
pass by Detroit each year on their way to the Mississippi or Atlantic
flyways.
        —*Nature Conservancy* magazine

The raptors are cruising
   the city, hanging with gangs—
the raptors'-in-training
   own damned angels, guardians
against kindness and
   uninvited dangers of light:

the way an explosion of sun
   on a junkyard bumper
can trigger memory, spinning
   a child into view who laughed,
once, into a camera's flash.
   The raptors distract, swoop down,
smother the glow to ash.

   Contrary to popular belief,
proud angels did not fall to hell,
   but soar, still. You can see them
by the millions above the city,
   unfurling a canopy of rust-dark wings,
watching with fierce and brilliant eyes
   over the not-quite-damned
who cling to craggy stoops,
   gathering for the kill.

The Robust Young Man Discusses His Burial
—curbside public phone, Manhattan

Five p.m. pause: the colors begin to meditate.
Even a red satin party pouf in the shop window
grows longer and subdued, an emperor's robe
gathering the shadows of a walled city. *I'd hate
to be buried in that place*, he says, resolute,
windbreaker flapping to show its lining of white net.
He pulls the tether, pacing—not in sneakers but dress
shoes perforated with small holes as if to refute
his own words, to affirm, *I breathe, I sweat.*
Is he quietly dying? Or could he be the type
who plans far ahead, a wheeler-dealer who invests
in real estate and burial plots at the best price.
I inch forward, finger my quarter (tails, heads),
until his eyes seize mine, alive enough to cut me dead,
and I give up waiting for that voice to interrupt—
to tell him, blasé as God, *Your time is up.*

Omega Train

I don't recall the faces
     of my fellow passengers
     huddled across the subway aisle
  in flight from a pointed gun—
fear pushing them from the last
     car to the first

(where they had to stop,
     having reached the beginning
and maybe the end);

I didn't think about the weight
     that rooted me, the river pressing
  the tunnel walls,
    and below the tunnel,
   the earth with its gaping mouth.

What I remember
     are the plastic turquoise seats,
  how hard, ugly,
and oddly bright they were,
  built for human cargo,
    and how they would outlast us all.

Dead Man Riding

The man sat on the subway for three hours before
passengers discovered his death.
                    —New York newspaper

I was invisible, slumped
          over as you are at the end
                    of the day: your faces slackened

into masks, previews
          of your last scene.
                    Others came and went

singly and in pairs but mostly
          in a mass like clods of earth breaking
                    apart and scattering

grit to the wind like all
          the people I've known no one
                    sticking around

for long everyone always
          going. In time you gathered
                    near, touched my wrist, lifted

me tenderly up while the two dimes left
          in my pocket rolled
                    away. Now it's me

gone borne on a silver pallet lifted
          up watching you ride
                    from dark to dark.

O Wanderers

They drag a queen-size mattress
into the subway car, laughing,
like Ulysses who's found his way.

A priest reading the Bible
looks up from his journey,
blinks, and looks away,
while another man lowers
a brown bag from his lips
to exclaim his wonder in tongues.

Posed against their backdrop
of blue-tufted, swaying sky,
the couple smile for a stranger's camera—
O beautiful, back-packing wanderers,
arms draped over their raft of happiness,
borne without fear onto this violent sea!

Keep Your Jewelry Safe
—a message from the NYC Transit Authority

Tuck your chains inside your clothing,
for you, passengers, are modern knights
evolved beyond chain-mail display;
illusionists skilled in the art of subterfuge,
causing their enemy to believe
the unadorned are poor as church mice.

Hide your chains because signs
of slavery attract bullies.
Conceal the facts:
your deep love
for that gold-linked noose,
your plan to exit at the next stop
to shop for thicker chains.

Keep your watches out of sight
because thieves steal time.
But the clock is the better thief,
filching years like pocket change,
commanding a great price
even on the street.

Turn your rings around
so the stones don't show.
The jewels may begin to fuse
to your body, a surprise weapon
like a hooked hand stuffed inside a coat.

Final caution: don't give to beggars here,
but to official, registered charities.
If you must give to supplicants,
press the stones into their open hands
so they'll know every gift exacts its price,
and the cost of taking what another owns
was once death by stoning.

Rapunzel Redux

She played rhythm and blues, hair
    'round her feet a hoop of fire
no one dared

come near. Village denizens
    adored her from afar,
whispering about childhood horrors:

that witch of a mother,
    years spent alone
locked in a room. Her song

was the rope she used to escape.
    It stretched miles across rivers,
reaching the Prince

of Kings Highway,
    who resolved to find her,
to climb that high, sweet sound.

I'll free you, he called out,
    pushing through the tavern.
I am free, she said, and signaled

her Merlin. Floodlights poured.
    Blinded, the Prince tripped
on Rapunzel's hair, then spent

the next decade in grief
    and wandering until he fell again,
this time for a shaved-head beauty.

The Load

A rope has appeared
outside my office window.

Sometimes it zigzags across the pane
like window wipers in a storm that say
Look harder or you'll die.
But then it drifts away and back
as if tied to a tree far below,
where a child sails through summer
on a rubber tire.

They say fall arrived awhile ago,
but from here, the season is a mere
abstraction. The only trees in view
are hulking evergreens on a rooftop terrace,
lined shoulder to shoulder
like secret service agents,
eyes trained on the street.

Now the rope shakes
as it lowers a bulging, man-sized sack.
The trees, intrigued, lean forward,
then shrug, stinging the dusky air.

A stranger phones to gloat
Bodies from the top-floor suite.
But Muzak from the ceiling sings
Christmas gifts for the child.

I've looked hard,
but I can only see so far,
and there are no clues—
not out there,
where clouds scowl shadows
across the face of white brick.
And surely not in here,

where the rooms next door,
around the corner, across the hall
have long been locked
and emptied.

An American Classic

We lay near the edge,
four friends on a tenement rooftop
above Manhattan's tip
and watched the red light blink,
staking a new place in the sky
where the day's work
on the first Twin had paused.

We never could find Gemini,
but that red light was our rising star,
and we kept returning summer nights
as Gatsby did to the green light
across the water. He heard laughter
clear as the clink of crystal goblets,
voices like money drifting near,
and stood alone, yearning.

We wanted none of that—power, money,
a way to remake ourselves—
wanted only to possess the moment,
touching plastic cups of wine
one to another, passing a joint around.
Each inhalation sparked a small fire
of wonder that our lives lay before us,
then mellowed to a softer light.

The steel skeleton stretched and grew,
heartless within
(years later, nearly crushing one of us
to dust). The red light climbed.
By summer's end, that pulse
of boundless aspiration
was mere backdrop to our conversation,
someone else's beacon or warning.

Landings

—*afternoon by an airport, New York City, 9/3/01*

In a gritty field not meant for play,
we taught our friend Vladimir
how to pitch and catch,
our jackets on the littered grass
wrapped in black plastic bags
that crackled like bales of hay
in every breeze of summer's end,

until I felt we'd become
a Norman Rockwell painting.
"Let's name it *Labor Day Baseball—
An American Pastoral,*"
the new citizen said in the same accent
we used to fear,
ducking under our grade school desks,
practicing for nuclear winter.

Just then the jets appeared
to sabotage our fun,
lowering their bodies so close,
we could count their rivets,
inspect the seams that gleamed
like a fighter's scars. Every other minute
another roar to shake the dead,

another pilot scraping our heads
until we had to shrug,
eclipsed by wings
more powerful than myth,
a brilliance that could crush
but passed us by.

The Fruited Plain
—*at a Korean greengrocer's, Jackson Heights, Queens, NYC*

The purple mountains are so high,
our hands must climb to reach
the top, the plum at its peak
of perfection. Once there, we strive

for more. No surprise—desire is why we came,
and this fruited plain knows no fence,
pushing out to sidewalk shoppers intent
on seizing the best. We sniff, squeeze, exclaim

to companions in Farsi, French, English, Urdu,
Spanish, Cantonese, Korean, Russian, Creole.
By the cash register, a sign extols:
We Will Never Forget. Citrus wear the tattoos

of corporations. Aztec-faced men build pyramid
displays, unpack papayas, their arms branded
with hearts and names of loved ones stranded
south of desert borders. At ten p.m., they sweep up fetid

remains, vanishing into a back room
with plastic buckets of unsold bouquets.
At eight, Kim and her brother, Sam, raise the steel gate
again on amber waves of ginger, bins stacked

with aloe huge as oars, tofu squares afloat. Kim knows
how plants can keep her customers well or steer
them back to health—the Irish supers; women who peer
from burkas; spike-heeled retirees; Croatian

carpenters; turbaned Sikhs with flag pins
on their suits. Proud to Be American from sea
to shining sea of blueberries, blood oranges, kiwi,
yams, yucca, mangoes, guava, pumpkins

that teachers at P.S. 69 will buy and soon carve
for the children, their grinning faces also lit
from within. They'll dress like goblins, learn the Holy Writ:
United We Stand. This is America. No one starves.

Eclipse

The full moon shrinks

to a crescent

in the space of moments.

What is left

is the red shadow of our planet

crossing the moon.

Shadow of clay canyon

and redwood,

shadow of fire

and city light—

His wide-open mouth closes

down to a thin-lipped grin

then a frown.

She slams the door, he shuts the light,

sits alone, away from the window,

mulling over what just happened.

The yellow sodium lamp goes dark

after years of smearing the street

the color of fear. With every sense he feels

the green traffic signal click on, click

and spark of her heels, tap

that sears his door—

all that makes us open wide,

beaming, say aah say yes,

and she enters

the hot dark pulse of us.

Underground Messengers

This Mercury bears the letter
X on his shaved skull;
his feet, bearing the swoosh of air-
pillowed sneakers, won't budge
an inch for anyone.
Fear Kills booms his drum-
skin of black t-shirt
on shoulder blades fierce
as wings. I read much in a trail
of fast-food crumbs: lost kids'
planted clues, bright orange
to catch the eye. Now sharp sounds
from unseen mouths are carving
hieroglyphs in the tunnel.
A man twists to whisper,
his words fluttering like pigeons
in the face of the woman
beside him. Is the flicker
that quickens, then goes dead
in her eyes, a sign
of anything? *We have a red signal
against us,* someone picks out
from the static, grandly interpreting
for all. Those of us who stand,
sway to Calypso from the car's far end.
Others nod in sleep, opening messages
washed up on warm, familiar shores.

Note

"Resurrection in an Initial 'R'": The painted letters in Renaissance Choir Books marked the first musically elaborate chant of a feast day. Inside a letter, artists painted scenes inspired by the event commemorated on that day. The initial "R" depicts the Resurrection of Easter.

The Robert McGovern Publication Prize is awarded to poets over 40 who have published no more than one book. The prize is established in memory of Robert McGovern, poet, professor, co-founder of the Ashland Poetry Press, and long-time chair of the English Department at Ashland University. Manuscripts are submitted by nomination only. The McGovern nominating panel currently consists of Alice Fulton, Andrew Hudgins, Philip Levine, Robert Phillips, Eamon Grennan, William Heyen, John Kinsella, Annie Finch, Carolyn Forché, Vern Rutsala, Richard Jackson, Gregory Wolfe and Gerry LaFemina. The co-winners of the 2005 McGovern Prize are as follows:

Maria Terrone, for *A Secret Room in Fall* (nominated by
　　Gerry LaFemina)
Nathalie F. Anderson, for *Crawlers* (nominated by Eamon
　　Grennan)

Former winners of the McGovern Prize:

A.V. Christie, for *The Housing* (nominated by Eamon Grennan)
Jerry Harp, for *Gatherings* (nominated by John Kinsella)